Zoobooks™

WHALES

Whales live in the ocean like fish. They swim around and hunt in the ocean like fish. They even look something like fish. But whales are NOT fish. They are mammals, the same as we are.

A mammal is an animal that has lungs and breathes air. It is warm-blooded, with a body temperature that is more or less the same all the time. The babies of mammals are born alive instead of hatched from eggs. (The exceptions to this rule are the primitive echidna and platypus—mammals that hatch from leathery eggs.) All mammal babies take milk from their mothers. Whales are sea mammals—mammals that live in the sea.

All whales, dolphins, and porpoises are known as *cetaceans* (see-**tay**-shuhnz), because they belong to a large group called the Cetacea. Cetaceans are divided into the toothed whales and the *baleen* (bay-**leen**) whales. Instead of teeth, baleen whales have brushes! The toothed whales are divided into six separate families. Killer whales, Pilot whales, and dolphins (all toothed whales) belong to one of these families—Delphinidae (dell-**fin**-uh-dee). The baleen whales are divided into three families.

In both the toothed whales and the baleen whales, males are called bulls, and females are cows. A young whale is called a calf.

BOTTLENOSE DOLPHINS
Tursiops truncatus

PYGMY SPERM WHALE
Kogia breviceps

SPERM WHALE
Physeter macrocephalus

RIGHT WHALE
Eubalaena glacialis

PYGMY RIGHT WHALE
Caperea marginata

'S PORPOISE
noides dalli

TLENOSE WHALE
Hyperoodon sp.

FIN WHALE AND CALF
Balaenoptera physalus

e Whale

l baleen whale. Grows to 30 feet and 20,000 pounds. Eats plankton and fish.
y found in coastal waters.

hal

ed whale that is the unicorn of the sea. Males have a single, spiraled tusk that
as long as 8 feet. Maximum body length is 16 feet. Males may weigh up to 3,500
s. Narwhals live year-round in the deep waters of the Arctic, feeding on fish,
shrimp, and crab.

Whale

are two species of this toothed whale. The long-finned pilot whale is only
y larger than the short-finned pilot whale. They are both about 20 feet long and
about 6,500 to 7,000 pounds. They herd in numbers of several hundred. Diet is
nd small fish.

Pygmy Right Whale

The smallest of the baleen whales. Maximum length is 20 feet. Maximum weight is
10,000 pounds. Subsists on plankton.

Pygmy Sperm Whale

A toothed whale. Maximum length is 11 feet. May reach 1,000 pounds or more.
Lives in the deep waters of the open ocean. Eats octopus, squid, and small fish.

Right Whale

A large baleen whale. Occasionally reaches 58 feet and may approach 200,000 pounds.
Eats plankton and prefers shallow waters. These playful whales sometimes raise their
flukes to use as sails, so the wind pushes them through the water.

Risso's Dolphin

A toothed whale that is among the largest of the dolphins, at 14 feet long and 1,500
pounds. Eats squid and small fish. They live in tropical and temperate waters worldwide.

Sound travels very fast in water. It can travel almost a mile in one second. For this reason, a whale can "see" a school of fish almost a mile away in only two seconds. (It takes one second for the sound to travel to the fish, and one second for it to travel back to the whale.)

Scientific tests show that toothed whales can do wonderful things with echolocation. Dolphins can tell one shape from another, even in muddy water or in complete darkness. They can tell a circle from a triangle, or a smaller circle from a larger circle. More important for the dolphin, when given the choice of two fish of the same size and shape, dolphins are able to tell by echolocation which fish they like to eat.

3

The sound comes back to the whale. If it takes a long time for the click to go out and come back, the whale knows the fish are far away. If it takes a short time, the whale knows the fish are close.

Dolphins can even tell what something made of without touching it or using th eyes. From 100 feet away, blindfolded dolphins can tell if a square is made of metal, wood, or plastic.

The water in the ocean is layered, like the layers on a cake. Some layers are warmer and some are colder, and some carry sound better than others. Whales seem to be able to use the best sound-carrying layers to "talk" to each other over very long distances. Fin whales can send out sounds that might be heard *more than 2,000 miles away*. In theory, it may be possible for whales on opposite sides of the Pacific Ocean to keep in touch with each other.

Baleen whales can be very big. The largest of them, the Blue whale, can reach 100 feet or more. There are baleen whales that are much smaller. Some never grow any longer than 20 feet—smaller than a newborn Blue whale!

It is not size that determines which whales belong to this group. It is the way they catch their food. All baleen whales filter, or strain, tiny plants and animals from seawater. Sometimes they may catch small fish, but they mostly filter the small organisms known as plankton. In certain parts of the ocean, billions of tiny plankton float near the water's surface, and baleen whales go there to feed.

Blue whales are the bigges animals that have ever live on earth. They are over si times bigger than the biggest dinosaur eve found. They make elephants look reall small. A Blue whale can weigh as much as *32 elephants*.

The two "wings" on the end of a whale's tail are called flukes (flookz). When a whale swims, the flukes push against the water to propel the whale. People often wear swim fins, or flippers, for the same purpose. For an animal as big as a whale, the flukes must be very sturdy. Strong fibers are densely packed inside the flukes to make them almost as strong as steel.

All the power for pushing a whale forward comes from its tail. For this reason, the muscles in the tail are the largest in a whale's body. Think of the power it must take to push a 300,000-pound whale through the water!

BLOWHOLE

LUNGS

Whales are mammals so they must breathe air. They can dive under the water, but they must always return to the surface for air. Rather than breathing through nostrils where your nose would be, a whale takes in oxygen through its blowhole—on top of its head. This way, the whale can breathe without coming very far out of the water.

BLUBBER

WARM

COLD WATER

Whales often swim in very cold water. To help them stay warm, they have a thick layer of fat around their bodies. This is called *blubber*. It acts like an overcoat to keep heat inside the body from escaping.

A human skeleton usually weighs less than 25 pounds. The skeleton of a Blue whale can weigh more than *50,000 pounds*.

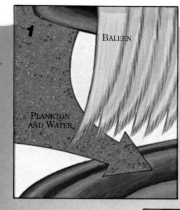

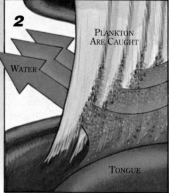

The baleen in a whale's mouth hangs down like the teeth of a comb. The pieces of baleen overlap a little and are fringed along one side. When a gulper feeds, water and plankton are sucked into the mouth ①. Then the throat contracts, pushing the tongue up. This forces the water out through the baleen ②. The plankton are caught on the fringed edges of the baleen and swallowed.

...e baleen whales
... by sifting plankton directly out of the water.
... swim close to the surface with their mouths
...n. Plankton float into the mouth and are
...ght on the baleen, a horny substance also
...d whalebone. These whales are
...d "skimmers" because that
...ow they feed.

Other baleen whales are called "gulpers" because they feed by gulping huge amounts of water and plankton into their mouths. Their pleated throats bulge out to hold it all. (To see what happens next, look at the diagrams at right.)

Isn't it surprising that the largest animals on earth survive by eating some of the smallest organisms on earth? A Blue whale may actually be *100 million times larger* than the plankton it eats.

The largest of the plankton is called krill (above). Krill may grow to be two inches long. Most types of plankton are much smaller. Some are so small that you would need a magnifying glass to see them.

A large Blue whale can eat more than 9,000 pounds of food a day. Every time it swallows, more than 100 pounds of food can go down its enormous throat.

...'s
... are used
...ring. On the
... they are smooth
...nded like paddles.

WHALE FLIPPER

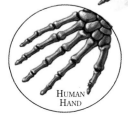

HUMAN HAND

Inside, the bones look very much like the bones of your fingers. Blue whales have only four of these "fingers," but most whales have five.

The bodies of toothed whales are usually darker on top and lighter underneath. This is called counter-shading and makes the whales harder to see in the water. When the whales hunt, counter-shading makes it possible for them to "sneak up" on their prey. The prey animals don't see the whales until is too late.

The pictures at left show how counter-shading works. When the whale is seen from below ①, its light-colored belly blends with the sunlight sparkl on the water's surface. When seen from above ②, the dark back blends with the darkness of the de water below.

1

2

In some ways, whales look like fish, but a whale's body is very different from a fish's body. For one thing, the whale is covered with skin instead of scales. The skin is smooth and firm. If you touch it, it feels like soft rubber.

Some toothed whales have tremendous swimming power for their size. Their muscles give them enough power to leap high into the air. A Killer whale weighing 12,000 pounds can actually jump more than 20 feet into the air.

All toothed whales have five bony "fingers" inside their flippers.

4

Whales and fish swim differently. Fish move tails from side to side. Whales move their tai flukes, up and down. The upward stroke prov most of the power to drive the whale forward For this reason, it is called the power stroke.

The teeth of toothed whales reflect the size and type of prey the whale must catch. Killer whales sometimes catch large sea mammals like seals and walruses. Killer whale teeth are thick and heavy.

The Bottlenose dolphin (left) eats small, slippery fish. To hold its prey, it has as many as 100 sharp little teeth. The False Killer whale (right) has larger and fewer teeth to catch larger fish and squid.

Sperm whales, the biggest toothed whales, have the biggest teeth to catch the biggest prey. All of their teeth are in the lower jaw. When the whale closes its mouth, the teeth fit into sockets in the upper jaw.

One big difference between toothed whales and baleen whales is how they eat their food. Baleen whales swallow lots of small animals at one time. Toothed whales catch and swallow bigger animals *one at a time*. Like baleen whales, toothed whales don't chew their food—they swallow it whole. A Killer whale can swallow about 50 pounds of food at one time.

Toothed whales are much smaller, as a rule, than baleen whales. The largest of the toothed whales, the Sperm whale, grows to a length of about 60 feet, and the Killer whale can reach 32 feet. Most toothed whales are between 10 and 20 feet long. The smallest of the toothed whales measures only 3 feet.

The difference in size between toothed whales and baleen whales may have to do with the ways that the two groups get their food. Baleen whales don't have to be fast to feed themselves. They just cruise along gathering up plankton. Toothed whales must chase their prey. Excessive size could slow them down.

Most toothed whales are excellent hunters. They often work in groups to round up prey in the same way that lions or wolves cooperate when they hunt. Groups of Killer whales have been known to attack Polar bears and Blue whales.

LONG-FINNED PILOT WHALES
Globicephala melaena

HUMPBACK WHALE
Megaptera novaeangliae

BLUE WHALE
Balaenoptera muscu

ROUGH-TOOTHED DOLPHIN
Steno bredanensis

BOWHEAD WHLAE
Balaena mysticetus

RUSSO'S DOLPHIN
Grampus griseus

CHINESE RIVER DOLPHIN
Lipotes vexillifer

Cuvier's Beaked Whale
A toothed whale of some size. Maximum length is 23 feet. Maximum weight is 10,000 pounds. These whales live in deep water—often near sea canyons—where they eat squid and deep-water fish. Named for Georges Cuvier, noted French biologist of the early 19th century.

Dall's Porpoise
A small toothed whale. Reaches a length of 7 feet and a weight of 350 pounds. Eats fish and squid. Named after William Healey Dall, who collected the first specimen for science.

False Killer Whale
A toothed whale. Maximum length is 20 feet. Maximum weight is 4,800 pounds. The resemblance to a killer whale is slight. Diet is fish and squid.

Fin Whale
The second largest whale. A baleen whale. Maximum length is 88 feet. Maximum weight is 161,000 pounds. Feeds on small crustaceans and small pelagic fish.

Gray Whale
A baleen whale of rather large size. Can reach 50 feet and 56,000 pounds. Gray hug the coastline and occupy coastal lagoons during their 6,000- to 7,000-mile This is the longest migration known for a mammal. They are bottom feeders, ea plankton and small fish.

Humpback Whale
A large baleen whale with large flippers—the longest of any cetacean. This wh attains a maximum length of 62 feet—its flippers are one-third this length. Humpbacks can weigh as much as 106,000 pounds. Males are known for their "songs" during breeding season.

Killer Whale
A large toothed whale. Maximum length is 32 feet. Maximum weight is 18,000 Killer whales hunt in packs to eat fish, birds, sea turtles, and marine mammals including other whales.

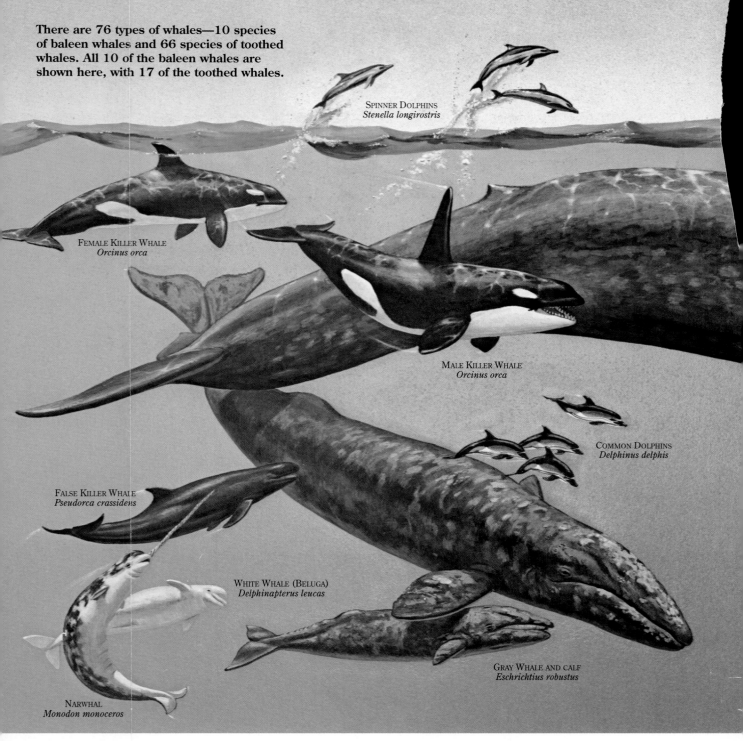

There are 76 types of whales—10 species of baleen whales and 66 species of toothed whales. All 10 of the baleen whales are shown here, with 17 of the toothed whales.

SPINNER DOLPHINS
Stenella longirostris

FEMALE KILLER WHALE
Orcinus orca

MALE KILLER WHALE
Orcinus orca

COMMON DOLPHINS
Delphinus delphis

FALSE KILLER WHALE
Pseudorca crassidens

WHITE WHALE (BELUGA)
Delphinapterus leucas

GRAY WHALE AND CALF
Eschrichtius robustus

NARWHAL
Monodon monoceros

Baird's Beaked Whale
A large toothed whale. Maximum length is 40 feet. Maximum weight is 24,000 pounds. Eats squid and fish. Lives in ocean and coastal waters.

Blue Whale
A baleen whale. Largest of all whales, earning the name leviathan because of its enormous size. Record length is 110 feet. Record weight is 418,000 pounds. Normally weigh 220,000 to 300,000 pounds and reach a length of 85 to 90 feet. Eats plankton. Usually found in deep waters.

Bottlenose Dolphin
This toothed whale gets its name from its long beak, which looks something like the neck on a bottle. Reaches length of 13 feet and weight of 1,450 pounds. Eats fish, shrimp, and eels.

Bottlenose Whale
A large toothed whale. Known to reach 32 feet. May weigh as much as 18,000 pounds. These whales are deep divers and may stay underwater for an hour. They eat squid.

Bowhead Whale
One of the largest baleen whales, reaching a length of 50 feet or more. May weigh 133,000 pounds. This whale got its name from whalers who thought the huge head looked like the bow, or prow, of a ship. Bowheads eat plankton. They are found in the cold waters of the Arctic Ocean.

Bryde's Whale
A baleen whale of medium size. Maximum length is 50 feet. Maximum weight is 44,000 pounds. Eats small fish. Found in both deep water and in shallow coastal waters. Named for Captain Johan Bryde, who established South Africa's first whaling station.

Common Dolphin
This toothed whale is common in all the oceans of the world. Maximum length is 8 feet. Maximum weight is 300 pounds. Feeds on squid and schools of migrating fish. Often congregates in herds of 2,000 to 3,000 individuals.

All whales dive beneath the surface of the water, but to varying depths and for different periods of time. To prepare for diving, they take several deep breaths. This clears their lungs and builds up a store of extra oxygen in their blood. Whales also store extra oxygen in their muscles.

Most whales don't dive very deep, and they don't stay under the water for very long before they come back up for air. Sperm whales, though, can stay underwater for more than an hour and may sometimes dive to a depth of almost two miles!

The Bottlenose dolphin is the toothed whale that is most often seen in aquatic parks. When it streaks around a pool and leaps through the air, it seems incredibly fast and graceful. But it is not even close to being the fastest of the whales. The top speed for a Bottlenose is about 18 miles per hour. A killer whale in the wild has been timed at 34½ miles per hour.

Far below the surface of the sea, Sperm whales find one of their favorite foods—giant squid. These huge sea monsters are as long as the whales that hunt them. Imagine the battle that must take place in the ocean's depths between these two giants of the sea.

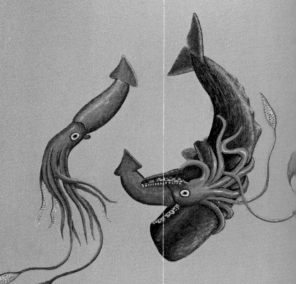

Toothed whales can "see" with their ears. If you have ever tried to open your eyes in the ocean, you know why whales really can't depend on their eyes to find their way around. Even in "clear" water, you can't see much farther than 200 feet. The deeper you go beneath the surface, the less light there is. At a depth of 1,300 feet, the ocean is pitch black.

Luckily for those whales that must hunt their food, water carries sound better than it carries light. Sound travels more than four times faster in water than it does in air—and it travels farther. Some whales have been able to take advantage of this and can "see" with sound. The process is called echolocation. The whales that use echolocation to navigate and find food "see" much farther underwater than you can see in air! Humans developed sonar (Sound Navigation Ranging) to do what whales that use echolocation do naturally!

1
To "see" what lies ahead of it in the dark ocean, a whale sends out a sharp, clicking sound.

A
The clicking sounds that toothed whales use for echolocation may come from air spaces (called air sacs) inside the head. Air may be forced back and forth very fast in the sacs to make the clicks.

2
Some distance away, the click hits a school of fish and bounces back, like a ball bouncing off a wall. The echo of the click starts traveling back toward the whale.

B
The sounds move forward through a space in the whale's forehead. This space is called the melon.

SOUND STARTS HERE

MELON

C
The melon is filled with oil. Some scientists believe that the oil focuses the sounds into a more powerful beam—like a magnifying glass focuses the rays of the sun.

JAWBONE

INNER EAR

E
The sounds enter the jawbone and travel along an oil-filled channel to the inner ear. The arrow shows the path that the sounds probably take.

D
When the sounds return, the whale may hear them in a very peculiar way. The outer ears of whales are not in a good position to hear sounds coming from the front, and a whale's ears are often partly plugged. A whale may pick up the vibrating sound waves through its *jawbone*.

CUVIER'S BEAKED WHALE
Ziphius cavirostris

SEI WHALE
Balaenoptera borealis

BRYDE'S WHALE
Balaenoptera edeni

MINKE WHALE
Balaenoptera acutorostrata

BAIRD'S BEAKED WHALE
Berardius bairdii

Rough-toothed Dolphin

A small toothed whale—9 feet long, 350 pounds. These are sociable animals that like to ride the waves of passing ships. They eat small fish, octopus, and squid.

Sei Whale

A large baleen whale. Females are larger than males and may grow to more than 65 feet and weigh 53,000 pounds. Plankton and small schooling fish make up the diet. The whales scoop up these fish easily, because Sei whales can swim at 24 miles per hour or more.

Sperm Whale

The largest of the toothed whales, at 60 feet and 100,000 pounds. Its large head takes up nearly one-third of its length. Sperm whales are believed to live as long as 70 years. They prefer to eat giant squid, but will also take octopus, sharks, and fish. They often feed at depths of 3,000 feet or more.

Spinner Dolphin

A small toothed whale. The largest spinner dolphins may reach 7 feet and 200 pounds. These acrobatic whales leap out of the water and somersault in the air—as their name suggests. Squid and fish form their diet.

White Whale (Beluga)

A toothed whale noted for its creamy white skin. Reaches about 16 feet and weighs about 2,500 pounds. Prefers shallow waters of the Arctic Ocean—sometimes seen in estuaries and rivers. Highly vocal, they squeal and chirp and are sometimes called "sea canaries." They feed on fish, squid, and crab.

Chinese River Dolphin

A small toothed whale found only in China. Grows to about 8 feet and 180 pounds. One of several species of toothed whales that live in fresh water. They eat catfish and other bottom-dwelling river creatures.

Sometimes, whales are stranded on a beach and die. For no apparent reason, a group of whales may swim into shallow water near a beach. When the tide goes out, they are left high and dry. Nobody is sure why these mass strandings occur, but some scientists feel that the echolocation systems of the whales may not be working correctly. As a result of this, the whales may become confused about where they are, and swim into shallow waters that they would usually avoid.

In addition to finding food, whales probably use echolocation for finding their way around in the ocean. When a whale is close to land, the ability to see what's ahead is particularly important. By sending out clicks, a whale can probably tell when it is too close to rocks or other dangerous places.

Are whales intelligent? There are some scientists who feel that some types of whales may be as intelligent as people. There are a few scientists who believe that whales may be more intelligent than people.

A lot of facts have been collected about whale intelligence—but it's hard to decide what the facts really mean. For example, some whales have very large brains. The Sperm whale has the largest brain of any animal that has ever lived. It can weigh as much as 20 pounds—four times more than the largest human brain.

Does size tell us how good a brain is? Among humans, Albert Einstein probably had the best brain of all. But Einstein's brain was not the largest human brain.

What about the structure of a whale's brain? Can this tell us anything about a brain's ability? Scientists have studied human brains and found that certain parts of the brain are related to certain kinds of activity. The front part of the brain, for example, has to do with thinking.

The front part of many whale brains is very large. Some dolphins have many more brain cells in this area than humans do. We don't know whether they use them for thinking, or for something we can't even imagine.

This is the main problem in trying to say how intelligent whales may be. Their lives are so different from ours that they need a different kind of intelligence than humans do.

If humans ever do learn to "talk" with whales, we may learn that whales are neither more nor less intelligent than we are. They are simply fully adapted to a life that is different than ours.

DOLPHIN BRAIN   HUMAN BRAIN

Some scientists believe that the amount of folding on the front part of the brain shows the amount of intelligence that a creature has. Dolphins have twice as many folds as people do.

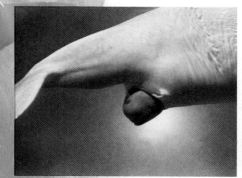

Baby whales are born differently from almost all other mammals. They are born underwater. As soon as the newborn whale emerges, the mother helps her youngster to the surface for its first breath.

A young whale stays close to its mother. Shortly after birth it starts to take milk from its mother, just like all mammals. The milk is very rich, and baby whales grow very fast. During the first seven months after birth, a Blue whale can gain about *33,000 pounds*. It can gain weight at a rate of 10 pounds an hour!

y people have seen whales trying to
 other whales. A group of dolphins will
etimes work together to keep the
hole of a sick dolphin above water so
n continue to breathe. If the dolphin's
hole were allowed to slip under the
r, the dolphin would drown. Some
ntists say this is intelligent social
avior. Others say it is simply instinct.

Some whales seem to do very "intelligent" things when they feed. Humpback whales sometimes catch krill or fish in a "bubble net." One or two whales swim in a circle around a school of fish. As they swim, they blow bubbles. The bubbles frighten the fish, and they flee to the center of the circle. Then the Humpbacks simply swim up the middle of the bubble net and swallow most of the fish.

The ability to learn by imitating others is often considered to be a sign of intelligence. Dolphins, Killer whales, and other toothed whales are famous for their ability to learn and perform tricks. Often, when they are bored, they make up new tricks of their own.

Many types of whales are close to extinction, including the Blue whale and other large whales. For hundreds of years, people have hunted and killed whales for their meat and oil. Endangered whales are protected by the Marine Mammal Protection Act in the United States, and the International Whaling Commission also offers some protection. Many countries still ignore the laws designed to save the whales. Today there are better sources for oil and meat that don't require the killing of whales. But conservation is a complex problem. People whose only livelihood is whaling oppose protecting whales. Until those people learn other methods for earning a living, whales will continue to be killed. Many organizations work to protect endangered whales. Some of them are listed here.

HUMPBACK WHALES